# WILD SURRENDER

## Also by r.h. Sin

*Whiskey Words & a Shovel*

*Whiskey Words & a Shovel II*

*Whiskey Words & a Shovel III*

*Rest in the Mourning*

*A Beautiful Composition of Broken*

*Algedonic*

*Planting Gardens in Graves*

*Planting Gardens in Graves Volume Two*

*Planting Gardens in Graves Volume Three*

*She Felt Like Feeling Nothing*

*Empty Bottles Full of Stories*

*She Just Wants to Forget*

*Falling Toward the Moon*

*We Hope This Reaches You in Time*

*A Crowded Loneliness*

*She's Strong, but She's Tired*

*She Fits Inside These Words*

*Winter Roses after Fall*

*Dream, My Child*

*Anywho, I Love You*

*I Hope She Finds This*

*I Hope This Reaches Her in Time Revised Edition*

*Come Back to Me*

*This Day Is Dark*

*Beautiful Sad Eyes, Weary Waiting for Love*

*Ascending Assertion*

*A Midnight Moon*

*Read This If You've Been Ghosted*

*The Year of Letting Go*

*New Moons*

*My Dear Wildflower*

*Serenity's Song*

*The Quiet After*

*She Outgrew the Wound*

# WILD SURRENDER

*the fire*

r.h. Sin

Andrews McMeel
PUBLISHING®

The authorised representative in the EEA is
Simon and Schuster Netherlands BV,
Herculesplein 96 3584 AA Utrecht, Netherlands.
(info@simonandschuster.nl)

Andrews McMeel Publishing
a division of Andrews McMeel Universal
1130 Walnut Street, Kansas City, Missouri 64106
www.andrewsmcmeel.com

26 27 28 29 30 RLP 10 9 8 7 6 5 4 3 2 1

ISBN: 979-8-8816-1206-1

Library of Congress Control Number: 2026935532

Editor: Danys Mares
Art Director: Diane Marsh
Production Editor: Elizabeth A. Garcia
Production Manager: Shona Burns

FSC
www.fsc.org
MIX
Paper | Supporting responsible forestry
FSC® C102842

You looked into me
like I was made
of something holy
That was the moment
I began to believe it

Your hands spoke a language
older than sound

We didn't just fall in love
we rose into it
like smoke
finding its way
toward heaven

There is a fire
that does not burn
it reveals

You kissed me
like you
were remembering
something

Every time our eyes met
the air thickened
asking for more honesty

Your touch taught my skin
the difference between
being used and being worshipped

We moved slow
deep and intentional
because we knew
the night was watching

You touched my soul
through my body
and my body
answered with release

Desire is not
the opposite of peace
Sometimes
it's the doorway to it

You are the warmth
I didn't know I'd been starving for

When you breathed my name
the silence became sacred

I don't need the world
to understand us
The fire will do
all the explaining

Your love feels like a match
struck in a dark cathedral

She never needed
to ask permission
because she knew her life
would become like magic
the moment she gave herself over
to the rhythm
of her own pulse

You looked at me
and everything warm
inside me woke up

You didn't ask
you invited, and
my body answered
before I could think

Your voice slid under my skin
slow, certain, already home

The first time we kissed
the world bent around us
like metal in heat

Your teeth touched my neck
and my pulse went to confession

Your hands knew things
about me
I hadn't told myself

Every inch of you
was a question
I was born to answer

I felt your desire
like sunlight
steady, deliberate
impossible to hide

I didn't need to undress you
to make you come undone

Your stare was a match

My restraint, gasoline

I kissed your shoulder
like it was a story
I needed to finish

There was no sin
in that moment
only worship
disguised as need

You leaned in
and my whole history
went quiet

Every slow touch
felt like an answer
to a question my body
had been asking for years

I didn't need music
Your breath was the song
Your hips, a melody

# *the storm*

As your eyes meet this page, you understand fully that it begins in the quiet. The kind of silence where two souls start breathing in the same rhythm without realizing it. A glance, a shift in the air. A pause that stretches thin. You say something small, something innocent, but the way your mouth moves ruins my composure.

Every word after feels heavier, softer, closer. When your hand brushes mine, I feel it everywhere. The world tilts; my skin awakens.

I don't remember when the thought of you became a need, but here it is, alive in my throat, begging to be named. You move closer, and suddenly, nothing in me wants to be careful.

There is a moment before it happens, the point where want becomes gravity. Your eyes on mine, and I can feel the air thinning, asking for us to surrender.

I taste the edge of your breath, the almost of it. My pulse goes wild and offbeat.

You touch my jaw and the whole night exhales. We aren't speaking anymore.

It's not chaos; it's a ceremony.

Your hands teach me that worship doesn't need words.

You kiss me: slow, deliberate, a thief learning the lock.

Your tongue traces my name like it's been waiting for permission.

I press against you, and the air turns to fire.

There's no room left for thought.

Every inhale is you; every exhale is surrender. The taste of your skin becomes the only thing I believe in. We pull each other in, and your body arches toward the inevitable, trembling between prayer and explosion. It's a rhythm older than memory, a storm finding its thunder.

We lose the concept of control. The bed, the floor, the space between moments, all gone. Your breath catches, and mine follows. Every sound becomes confession. You move inside the heat, and I meet you with everything I am. There's no separation now, only pulse on pulse, need on need, wave on wave.

The world folds in half, and the light behind my eyes, warm, spilling over reason. This beautiful, ruinous moment when we both stop pretending to be anything but alive, in lust and in love.

There's a hunger
in the way she breathes
a whisper that turns silence
into sin

She writes her desires
in the language of patience
letting the night
translate her body
into a foreign tongue fluent
in every desire running through me

Her eyes don't look at you
they undress you
in a slow devotion

The moon watches her
like a jealous lover
wanting to touch
what only dreams can reach

She tastes like the truth—
sweet, forbidden
and impossible to forget

Her lips
don't speak
they confess

She isn't chaos
she's the invitation
to lose control

My name becomes prayer
when she says it
between breaths
before climax

Desire blooms
in her quiet
watered by thoughts
she never speaks aloud
growing into something
I'm eager to taste

Every touch
feels like a secret
you shouldn't know
but can't forget

Her light is holy
Her darkness is home

---

She is made of calm fire
the kind that warms
and ruins

I kissed her thoughts
before I ever touched her skin

Her silence
isn't empty
it's the sound of temptation
learning patience

The night bends
to the rhythm
of her thighs
moving toward ecstasy

My gaze
walks up her spine
and stays
She tastes like midnight
and a promise kept
My name on her tongue
turns into heat
She smiles and the room
forgets its manners

The bed learns
our favorite secret

Her fingertips
write scripture
on my throat
Between her breaths
the moon loses count
We practice silence
until it moans

She unbuttons worry
and hangs it on a chair
Her laughter
leaves bite marks
on the night
The mirror fogs
when she says
my name slowly
I drink her hunger
and never spill

Our shadows kiss
before we do

The city goes quiet
when she opens
her throat to my name

We make rain
without water

Her softness
is dangerous
in all the right ways

She keeps a key
under her tongue
for this room
I wear her perfume
like a bruise
We trade secrets
with our mouths
full of light
Her silence
drips sugar
on the floor

She says please
and everything
inside me kneels

Beneath her
looking at the midnight sky
I see the moon
learning the rhythm
of her spine
I write a million yeses
in the curve of her neck

I get lost in the country
of her skin
and refuse a map

We trade sleep
for warm waterfalls
and silky explosions

Her heartbeat
turns my hands
into believers

She wears my bite
like jewelry

I hold her hair
like a secret

Her taste rewrites

the night in my mouth

I beg for water

She gives me more fire

Her voice
pulls stars
out of their orbit
Her nails
keep score
on my back
I travel
from her mouth
to her mercy
I let her name bloom
between my lips
She ties my doubt
to the headboard
We make poetry
from our sweat

She collects
my promises
with her mouth

Her body writes the endings
then starts again

# *another round*

You tilt your chin
and the room
starts breathing for us

I learn your rhythm
by listening with my hands

You press into the moment
and everything within me hardens

I call you mine
and the night believes me

You wear want

like perfume

I can't stop inhaling

I meet your gaze
and it pulls the floor closer

I drink your breath
like it was meant for me

You open your silence wide
and it floods the room

I hold your wrists
and time forgets its manners

I learn your name
in every language of want

You tug my certainty
into something wilder

I taste the edge
of your self-control
and discover your honey

You let the soft
turn sharp
and I thank you for it

You arch
into a wild promise
and keep going

You tell me where
to find your *yes*
and then move it
to a place
too deep for hands

You pull my hunger
like a ribbon
through your teeth

You drag your nails
across my willpower

I kiss your pulse
until it forgets
how to behave

I map your heat
with a patient tongue

You ask for more
then hand me the match

I light your edges
and guard the flame

You ride the hard line

between

soft and savage

I anchor you
while you learn to float

You pour yourself
over the hour
and stain it
with wild honey

I take

your patience apart

with kindness

I make a home
where your breath breaks

I make your quiet
sing into my mouth

You keep saying, *Almost*

and I keep earning the rest

I let your needs
rearrange my priorities

I catch your moans
before the walls do

With a lash of my tongue
I thank your body
for telling me its truth

I push you
to the edge
and hold the railing

You let go in a way
that feels deliberate

I taste your relief
and keep it warm

My love
I yearn on purpose . . .
like striking a match
with my thoughts
and the idea of you

Pleasure gathers
where I keep believing

Then you look at me
and the room becomes heat . . .
and I'm caught inside it
burning slow
wanting more
asking for none of it back

You are the quiet
after the fire
the ache
that doesn't hurt anymore
the reason the night
forgives itself
There is no more wanting
only the echo of it
folded into the way
our hearts breathe
We came here to burn
and left here clean
soft again
wild still

The night begins in
*soft hunger.*